PARENTING

Written By:
Herbert I. Kavet

Illustrated By:
Martin Riskin

Ivory Tower Publishing Co., Inc.
125 Walnut Street
P.O. Box 9132
Watertown, MA 02272-9132
Telephone #: (617) 923-1111   Fax #: (617) 923-8839

Nobody wants the parenting job, but everyone thinks they can do it better than you.

"Adam, this is not what we mean by bonding."

Dad spends quality time with Jason.

"Melissa just picks at her food."

Toilet Training

There are over 1000 generally approved methods of Toilet Training. None of them work. Though you never believe it at the time, the day does finally arrive when you no longer have to feel guilty about filling your local dump with disposable diapers.

"Eric has always been a leader in his nursery school."

Driving With Kids

97% of all traffic accidents are caused by children distracting their parents while they're trying to drive. The other 3% are caused by drivers, driven to drink, again by their kids. The insurance companies get back at these kids by charging them (really you) exorbitant rates when they get their license.

"They HAVE been very quiet."

"Matthew just thought the fishies were hungry."

"He <u>does not</u> have to see a psychiatrist just because he'd rather play with Jennifer's doll."

The Informer

Every group of kids has an informer. This squealer or tattle tale, if you will, thinks he or she is ingratiating themselves with an adult by bearing tales of misdeeds.

It's the adult's job to maintain this source so they have access to good information without unduly nurturing this despicable habit.

"She said Luke was such a timid child."

"OH OH — 5 o'clock, time for the neglected-abandoned look."

"They haven't learned to pass yet."

Exhibitionists

We're all proud of our private parts and some people just like to advertise more than others. Kids are the same and simply because the advertising takes place in a supermarket or at nursery school it shouldn't surprise you. Who knows, it could lead to a great paying film career.

"No, I want my truck <u>AND</u> Ryan's truck."

"Jessica did not get more than you."

Every now and then, Cynthia recalled some of the
advantages of diapers.

Difference Between Little Girls And Little Boys

Little girls will pick up toys one at a time and play with them nicely.

Little boys will put all their toys together in the center of the room and jump up and down on them.

"Because I said so is a perfectly logical reason."

"All right, Tommy's in the club."

The Tooth Fairy

You can think what you like about the tooth fairy, but when the kids reach 11 or 12 you'll realize she was funded by your local orthodontist who is at this very moment planning to buy a new car with the income generated by those cute spaces in your child's mouth.

"Mom, Matthew ate all his Halloween Candy."

"OK, we're going to really find out
who hit whom first."

"Who ever told you such a ridiculous thing?"

Restaurants

Kids fall into three categories at restaurants:

1. They run around and bother other tables.
2. They hide under tables and poke at your feet.
3. The play with trucks on the table.

Each type has its advantage, but if you learn to pretend the kids who are running around causing everyone else to have indigestion are not yours, the dinner can be quite pleasant.

"They may laugh at your braces now, but when your teeth are all straight, they'll be jealous."

"Mrs. Feldspar, Weber left a puddle by the TV."

"I think Jordana's on the left near the back."

Bedtime Stories

If you read the story from books, your child will quickly memorize each page (though they still can't remember to flush the toilet) and read along with you. It's probably the same story every night which gets kind of boring for you but the kids love it. When you get a grandparent to put your son or daughter to bed and they do the story, they will have weeks of bragging with their friends over how their grandchild can already read.

Bedtime Stories

Made-up-as-you-go-along stories give you the flexibility to cut them short whenever you want and to tailor the story to the moral of the night.

"No, I'm not going to look again.
There's absolutely nothing under your bed."

"I told you to GO before we left."

Show And Tell

Do they still have show and tell at your kid's school? This diabolically clever activity was devised by teachers solely to give them another half hour to digest breakfast and allows practically inarticulate little kids to thoroughly embarrass their parents. It also gives teachers some great information to upstage you at teacher-parent conferences. "Oh, I just love that belly dancing outfit you have." It's a good idea to search the curious little creatures every morning to be sure your adult video cassettes and garter belt collection stay in your bedroom drawers.

"No, we're not there yet.
I <u>told</u> you it would take eight months."

"It's absolutely mortifying when
your parents come to every game."

"I hope Mom hears me."

Kids & TV

Kids that don't watch too much TV develop much better imagination. Here are five all time favorite games.

1. Paint the baby

2. Indian Campfire

3. Doctor – great old time favorite with the little boy or girl next door

4. Pretend drive Daddy's car

5. Restaurant – a complete 5 course meal will be prepared in your kitchen using only ingredients found in your backyard plus 3 NEIGHBORHOOD PETS.

"Well, you promised you'd take care
of the last one, too."

"How can he remember what's on 56 channels and forget to flush the toilet?"

"Well, my dad's computers are more powerful than your dad's."

Nutrition

My kids think the 4 major food groups are pizza, McDonalds, ice cream, and crispy. Eating something green means picking out that color M&M's. To get them to try something new, I need a taster standing by to prove it won't poison them. Incredibly, they'll eat things at a friend's house that would start a three day battle if served at home.

"We can't send the starving children your green peas because they have no refrigerator."

Nelson learns to use the computer at an early age.

"My mom says she works to make money for toys."

"Kyle's a day care center drop out."

"Who wants to sing 'Row, Row, Row Your Boat?'"

"I don't care what you saw, it's a beautiful day and you're playing outside."

Mom finally finds those string beans Ryan didn't
want to finish.

"But Mom, where do tomatoes really come from?"

"It's OK, Rachel, lots of children
throw up on swings."

"I told you they wouldn't let us do it."

Parental Retorts For Every Occasion

"We'll see"

This is a perfect response to any request that is either
a) completely ridiculous or
b) out of the realm of possibility.

"Maybe"

Use this word when "we'll see" doesn't work.
(Also a synonym for "no.")

Parental Retorts For Every Occasion

"If it's okay with your mother, it's okay with me"

This buck passer will relieve you of responsibility
for any of your child's hazardous activities such
as mountain climbing, hang gliding, or skate
boarding. It also has an extra advantage: if
anything does happen, you can blame your wife.

"Wait until your mother gets home"

This dual purpose phrase can be used when
a) you don't want to be the bad guy or
b) you aren't sure of what to do.

Parental Retorts For Every Occasion

"Don't talk back"
A good response when your child either
a) talks back or
b) makes a particularly good point.

"What do you know?"
A logical defense after your child has made
two particularly good points.

Parental Retorts For Every Occasion

"I've told you a million times"

Don't over use this one—your child may be keeping a count that will weaken your credibility.

"This is the last time I'm going to tell you"

Have a back-up plan ready for this one— if your child persists, you'll be left with nothing to say.

These other books are available at many fine stores.

#2350 Sailing. Using the head at night • Sex & Sailing • Monsters in the Ice Chest • How to look nautical in bars and much more nautical nonsense.

#2351 Computers. Where computers really are made • How to understand computer manuals without reading them • Sell your old $2,000,000 computer for $60 • Why computers are always lonely and much more solid state computer humor.

#2352 Cats. Living with cat hair • The advantages of kitty litter • Cats that fart • How to tell if you've got a fat cat.

#2353 Tennis. Where do lost balls go? • Winning the psychological game • Catching your breath • Perfecting wood shots.

#2354 Bowling. A book of bowling cartoons that covers: Score sheet cheaters • Boozers • Women who show off • Facing your team after a bad box and much more.

#2355 Parenting. Understanding the Tooth Fairy • 1000 ways to toilet train • Informers and tattle tales • Differences between little girls and little boys • And enough other information and laughs to make every parent wet their beds.

#2356 Fitness. T-shirts that will stop them from laughing at you • Earn big money with muscles • Sex and Fitness • Lose weight with laughter from this book.

#2357 Golf. Playing the psychological game • Going to the toilet in the rough • How to tell a real golfer • Some of the best golf cartoons ever printed.

#2358 Fishing. Handling 9" mosquitoes • Raising worms in your microwave oven • Neighborhood targets for fly casting practice • How to get on a first name basis with the Coast Guard plus even more.

#2359 Bathrooms. Why people love their bathroom • Great games to help pass the time on toilets • A frank discussion of bathroom odors • Plus lots of other stuff everyone out of diapers should know.

#2360 Biking. Why the wind is always against you • Why bike clothes are so tight • And lots of other stuff about what goes thunk, thunk, thunk when you pedal.

#2361 Running. How to "go" in the woods • Why running shoes cost more than sneakers • Keeping your lungs from bursting by letting the other guy talk.

Ivory Tower Publishing Co., Inc.   125 Walnut St., PO Box 9132, Watertown, MA 02272-9132
Telephone #: (617) 923-1111   Fax #: (617) 923-8839